A Journey with Trees

Hearing God's Voice in Life's Seasons

JOANNA MONTESINO

Illustrations and cover artwork by Joanna Montesino

Edited and formatted by Katie Erickson, KatieEricksonEditing.com.

ISBN: 979-8-9866473-0-2

For my mother, Josefina

With much love

Thank you for believing in me

Amid the urban I find the forest
A park!
With a grove of trees
How delightful!
I sit on a bench with shade
Take a deep breath
And another, and another.
I sit still and silent
Feel the gentle breeze cool my warm skin
I smile and say a grateful prayer:
Thank you for this peaceful moment
And your presence in your creation.

~ Joanna Montesino ~

Come with me on a journey of listening...

Contents

Introduction
1

The Gift of Tears
5

Trees and Birthdays
11

A Beautiful Death
17

The Enduring Oak
23

Blossoms of Hope
29

Epilogue: A Promised Harvest
35

Acknowledgements
39

Recommended Resources
41

About the Author
43

Notes
45

Introduction

Once in a while, I like going for a walk at a golf course called Glendoveer. The three-mile trail around the course is a favorite among fitness-minded folks living in the surrounding neighborhood. Based on the abundance of conifer trees flanking the golf course and the woodchip-covered trail, this area likely was once a forest. At a certain part of the trail, the course opens up to a meadow-like field, with bordering conifers in a V-formation. There's something about the openness of this green field that beckons the soul.

One August day, as I reached this meadow on my occasional walk, I was stunned by the brightness of the sunlight draping the "V" of trees. It made me think about the power of this light that penetrates everything. Almost everyone rejoices at the sun. Especially in places where it often rains like my city of Portland, people feel good and happy when the sun comes out after a cloudy day.

I believe the sun is a sign pointing to the source of light. According to the biblical narrative, the Creator God spoke light itself into existence (Genesis 1:3), and Jesus stated, "I am the light of the world" (John 8:12). Moreover, there is a promise of a future city that will have God himself as its light: "The city does not need the sun or the moon to shine on it, for the glory of God gives it light, and the Lamb is its lamp" (Revelation 21:23). I believe we will feel a deeper, fuller joy when this divine "sun" shines his glorious light on the earth and fully restores everything that has been marred and broken by sin and death. The biblical text describes this transformation as follows: "Then I saw a new heaven and a new earth... And I heard a loud voice from the throne saying, 'Look! God's dwelling place is now among people, and he will dwell with them.

They will be his people, and God himself will be with them and be their God. He will wipe every tear from their eyes. There will be no more death or mourning or crying or pain, for the old order of things has passed away.' He who was seated on the throne said, 'I am making everything new!'" (Revelation 21:1a, 3-5a).

I've often wondered, "Will there be seasons (namely winter, spring, summer, autumn) on this new earth?" Not surprisingly, I wondered this again while walking at Glendoveer. I believe God replied to my silent query because immediately this thought came to my mind: "There will be perpetual light," as well as this Scripture verse: "There will be no night there" (Revelation 21:25b). Although we can't be certain whether seasons will occur on this new earth, in that moment, I sensed God's Spirit tell me there are spiritual lessons to be gleaned in the natural world we currently inhabit. The Creator wants to reveal wisdom and truth to us in the various seasons, so that through these "aha moments," we would ultimately discover him.

Close your eyes for a moment and imagine yourself on a leisurely walk. You look up at the billowy clouds and feel your chest expand as you breathe in the cool, fresh air. It is the month of April and spring is in full bloom. After seeing a sign for a nearby park, you decide to go there. Dogwood trees line the paved trail that runs through the grassy park. Their pink four-petaled blossoms capture your eyes, while your ears catch a conversation between a father and his daughter sitting on a bench a few feet away from you. The preschool-aged girl points to a tree and asks, "Daddy, what do you call that tree?" You notice him smile at her and hear the pleasure in his voice as he answers her inquiry. The little girl becomes wide-eyed with wonder, mouthing a believing "Ohhh..."

Hold this scene in your mind as you read this book – a compilation of my "aha moments" with God over the years. As I engaged in candid conversations with this good and loving Father, he spoke transformative truths to me through his creation, particularly trees and the changes they undergo from one season to the next.

I invite you to come close and listen in. What are you hearing that resonates with your journey?

The Gift of Tears

One December weekend many years ago, I decided to participate in a workshop called Heart Change[i] after the repeated promptings of a caring friend who knew of certain struggles I had. The workshop began with the instructor talking about pain and the purpose it serves in our lives. Pain alerts us that something has gone wrong and needs to be addressed. It is much like the warning light that comes on when a vehicle or a household appliance needs attending to. But how often do we experience pain in our lives and we either minimize it or deny that there is something wrong that needs to change? Certainly, that was the case for me then. As I listened to the instructor, my mind was telling me, "Yes, this is true—I can have a proper perspective of my pain," but my heart was saying, "Pain is no fun—just take it away! I don't care what it's supposed to do in my life." I wanted to stop hurting, but I was afraid to face the source of the pain.

Later on, the instructor played a song called "Blessed Are the Tears."[ii] It reinforced what they taught about pain through the metaphor of cleansing. When we cry, it's good for our souls. Tears are like raindrops that fall on the windows of a house and wash away some of the dirt. For some reason, this image of my tears cleansing my soul stuck out to me. I kept thinking about it throughout the weekend-long workshop. However, I didn't fully comprehend it until weeks later.

New Year's Day came. When I woke up, my heart sensed a tug to spend time with God. Despite the cold and rain, I decided to go for a hike at Multnomah Falls, a popular place to visit in Portland. To my delight and surprise, the parking lot was not crowded, and the rain felt refreshing as I went up the mountain.

My thoughts turned to the trees along the trail and how dreary they looked with bare branches. I remember saying to myself, "My heart and life feel as bleak as these trees look." Then I said to God, "When will I stop grieving and crying? I feel like my life is winter… so dark, depressing, and full of pain." At one point, I looked up and noticed one particular tree branch silhouetted against the grey, misty sky. Despite its barrenness, there was actually some beauty to it. I sensed God telling me to stop walking and keep looking at this tree and its branches. As I paused, I heard God speaking to my heart. It wasn't an audible voice but distinct thoughts entering my mind:

You might feel like your life is winter right now – cold and bleak. But you know, life has seasons, just like the physical world I created. There is spring, summer, winter, and fall, a time and purpose for everything. Look at this tree. On the outside it looks dead, but inside it is teeming with life. It's busy regenerating itself. Pretty soon, winter will give way to spring, and these bare branches will burst out into new and fresh buds, blossoms, and leaves—the signs of life! In the same way, your sorrow will not last forever. You might feel like you're dead inside, with no hope; but I am doing something great in your inner being. I have the power to bring life out of the death and darkness that you are going through if you believe me and allow me to do my work in you. And see the rain? It nourishes and cleanses the earth. In the same way, I can and want to use your tears and your pain to transform you and bring beauty out of the brokenness of your heart and life.

On hearing this message, awe and hope filled my heart. I encountered God's presence in a very special and intimate way, and I left Multnomah Falls with a smile and a light spirit. A week or so later as I was driving, I tuned into the radio and heard a song called "Healing Rain."[iii] In that moment, I realized that hearing this song was God's way of confirming what he told me during my hike and also at Heart Change.

Rain, like tears, is a paradoxical spiritual metaphor. Not only does it symbolize heartache and troubles but healing as well. Rainy days may be a downer, but they are also beneficial. Without rain, we would not have water, which is vital for life. Having this perspective enables us to deal with our pain maturely and productively.

I started to understand that pain is a season in life. It doesn't have to be permanent unless we allow it to be. I also came to realize that I don't have to be afraid of experiencing pain or sorrow because it is an instrument in God's hands to heal and transform me – if I let him. Because we live in a broken world where every human being is capable of wounding another, pain is a reality; everyone experiences it. But by God's grace, pain can be redeemed. If we let it, pain can lead us into the very heart of God, who is not a stranger to pain himself. He is with us in our pain. We can experience healing and hope in and through our dark seasons because God suffered for us when his son Jesus died on a cross in our place. Through his death, we can receive forgiveness and wholeness. Scripture tells us, "[The Lord] heals the broken-hearted and binds up their wounds" (Psalm 147:3) and "Surely... he carried our sorrows... and by his wounds we are healed" (Isaiah 53:4a, 5b). As we experience being forgiven, we can then forgive our offenders – probably the hardest thing for any human being to do! But when we depend on Jesus, he gives us the power and desire to do the impossible.

For Reflection and Prayer:

Think about a painful season you have gone through. What lessons did you learn from it? How did it contribute to your growth as a human being?

If you have unresolved areas of grief or pain, what ideas or beliefs may have taken root in your mind that could be false and unproductive? What ideas have put you in emotional or spiritual bondage? Ask God to shed light on this and speak truth to you right now.

Is there anything you need forgiveness for? Anyone you need to forgive? Jesus is waiting for you to give these burdens to him. (The nature of forgiveness is often misunderstood. For in-depth teaching on this topic, check out "Recommended Resources" at the end of this book.)

Trees and Birthdays

It was the middle of June, and the sky was atypically clear. I decided to take advantage of the sunshine in Portland by going on a hike near Mount Hood. It was also my birthday, and I invited my friend Emily to be my companion. We decided to take the Hood River route and stop by the hip little town for some jewelry shopping. Afterwards, we continued on our way via Highway 35, which was a pleasant drive, dotted with cherry trees, fruit stands, and wineries.

Suddenly, the iconic mountain, bold and strong, appeared on the horizon. Emily and I could not contain our delight. We stopped on the gravel shoulder and took pictures. Every single time I see Mount Hood with its snow-covered body, slightly hooked tip, and symmetrically shaped cone, I stop in my tracks. Mountains, along with stars and redwood forests, are a reminder that there is someone greater than you and me, someone even more magnificent than the creation. The psalmist tells us, "The heavens declare the glory of God; the skies proclaim the works of his hands" (Psalm 19:1). That day, as I gazed at Mount Hood sitting far away against the canvas of a wide blue sky, it declared, "Look at me! And when you do, stand in awe of my maker, who is your maker too, and know that he loves you. He created me for you, that you may get a taste of his infinite beauty, kindness, and goodness."

The trail to Umbrella Falls was flanked by Douglas firs, ferns, wildflowers, Hosta-looking plants, and fallen trees. Sometimes these dead trees blocked the trail and we either had to climb over or crawl under them. Once in a while, Emily and I were startled by a creaking sound, like what an old wooden rocking chair makes when your grandma sits on it. After hearing the sound a few times, we discovered that it came from trees, trees that seemed old and dry, trees that were counting their days. I wondered, "If these trees could speak, what would they tell us?"

During our hike, I kept anticipating other hikers, but we didn't encounter a single soul. It felt a little eerie. For four or five hours, we two women carrying backpacks and occasionally squealing with pleasure at tiny waterfalls and trillium flowers, roamed a forest without seeing another live person. We were all alone in the midst of leaves, logs, mud, water, and even snow! Again, as I often do when I am immersed in nature, I looked for truths revealed by the silence and the beauty of my surroundings. In that moment, I recalled Scripture that describes creation yearning and groaning for the redemption of God's children (Romans 8:19-21). I then imagined the eyes of the forest eagerly looking on the people hiking among its trees. Both the trees and the hikers long for the same thing.

Deep in our souls, regardless of faith tradition, religious affiliation, or lack thereof, we human beings know intuitively that things are not quite what they should be. We long to be redeemed, to experience a sense of glory or a "happily ever after" to our lives. The forest and everything else in nature certainly give us a taste and a glimpse of this glory. Think about a time you were stopped in your tracks by a sunset, a field of wildflowers, or a snow-covered mountain peak. How did you feel? What longings flowed inside of you? That morning, I felt a longing for my time of refreshment and fun to last forever – for time to stand still. I even felt bad about those trees that were creaking and whose days were coming to an end.

I celebrated my 44th birthday in the Mount Hood National Forest. Throughout my life, I've befriended many Chinese people and learned that in their culture, numbers have meanings. The number four happens to be bad luck because the Chinese word for "four" has a similar sound as the word for "death." If I believed in this superstition, I would not have celebrated that particular birthday!

In reality though, all of us humans, especially in Western culture, tend to dread gaining another ring in our trunk. Getting older makes us feel vulnerable, like we're a day closer to death. If trees could give advice, they would say to us, "What a silly thought! Another ring means a grander existence – a richer history to present and a greater story to tell." It's all about perspective.

When a creaking tree finally does crack and crash to the ground, the human assumes decay and death. But no sooner than that old tree becomes a log that a fern sprouts out of this same log, and a carpet of moss adorns this same piece of wood. It is a paradox, wouldn't you say? It is a stunning picture of redemption. Scripture tells us that in God's kingdom, death gives way to life. "Therefore, we do not lose heart. Though outwardly we are wasting away, yet inwardly we are being renewed day by day. For our light and momentary troubles are achieving for us an eternal glory that far outweighs them all" (2 Corinthians 4:16-18). Meditate on this truth the next time another year rolls around!

For Reflection and Prayer:

Spend some unhurried time outdoors, whether the forest, the mountains, the beach, or even just your neighborhood park. Observe your surroundings and listen to what they, or God through them, may be saying to you. Bring a journal and a pen so that you can record your thoughts, impressions, and feelings.

Read Psalm 19. At first glance, it may seem odd that the psalmist talks about divine "precepts" (e.g., Scripture, prophetic revelation) after he talks about creation. What do the physical/natural world and spiritual truth have in common according to this psalm? In what ways do God's creation and God's word communicate with human beings? In what ways does our heart posture affect the way we encounter nature and spiritual truth?

A Beautiful Death

It was a perfect autumn day—the sun was out but you could feel a slight chill in the air. I had finished my usual Saturday afternoon chores and come 4:00 pm, I sensed God calling me to spend time with him. So off I went gladly, directing my car to Laurelhurst Park because it was close to my house. I decided to walk at a slow leisurely pace, letting my lungs fill with fresh oxygen and feeling the breeze sift my hair. As I lazily strolled along the wide paths dotted with other people walking, jogging, and bicycling, I contemplatively looked up at the old, tall, and very large trees. Whenever I am outdoors, I like to observe, listen, and wonder. It was only September, but many trees and shrubs were already displaying bright reds, yellows, and oranges. The last time I went to this park, I really enjoyed sitting on a rock with my journal and pen in hand, right in front of the man-made pond, so I wanted to go back there.

While walking on the trail along the pond, I saw a bush whose green leaves were tinged with red streaks. It looked interesting, so I stopped and examined a leaf more closely, touching the surface with my fingers. I asked God, in the same way that a child would ask her mom or dad, "What makes the leaves change colors?" I was genuinely curious about the science behind it. But rather than googling it, it was more natural for me to ask my Father, the Creator God. Immediately a thought came into my mind: "The leaves are preparing to die. And in the process of dying, they gain a new beauty, don't you agree?"

I was expecting a more scientific explanation, but it made total sense to me. So, I quietly replied back, "Yes, Papa, the leaves are absolutely gorgeous!"

Then he said, "In the same way, when you die to yourself, you gain a new beauty."

When I heard it, I was stunned and thought to myself, "Gosh, I was merely curious about what happens to the leaves, and God is bringing up deep spiritual stuff!" But because I have had a relationship with him for many years and know from experience that he is completely good and trustworthy, I couldn't help bowing my heart and spirit in agreement, even though the idea of dying to myself has always scared me.

Every time I read the gospels and get to the part where Jesus tells his apprentices, "If any want to become my followers, let them deny themselves and take up their cross and follow me" (Mark 8:34 RSV), I realize that Jesus was keeping it real. What leader wants half-hearted followers? Don't we ourselves admire the heroes in movies and novels who are willing to die for a cause they believed in? Yet, if we are honest, we would rather not have to die to ourselves but instead do what we want to do, even though we may call Jesus our "Lord." There have been significant times in my life when I surrendered my will, desires, and understanding to God and felt I had done enough. But that day by the pond, I sensed I had just scratched the surface. This act of trust has depths he wants me to plumb.

A year later, I went for another autumn day walk at Laurelhurst Park and I anticipated God speaking to me again. When I got there, however, I sensed he wanted me to let go of any expectations, so I tried to just enjoy the physical release of walking and breathing in the fresh air. At one point, while I was staring at a carpet of red, orange, and yellow leaves that had accumulated on the side of the trail, I heard the Lord say to me, "The many leaves on the ground are dead and will eventually disintegrate and get mixed into the soil, serving as nutrients. Like these leaves, I want to see many 'deaths' among my people, for when many die to themselves, they, too, will produce rich spiritual nutrients to impart to the world they live in."

What I heard reminded me of a passage in the gospel of John where Jesus says, "Unless a kernel of wheat falls into the ground and dies, it remains only a single seed. But if it dies, it produces many seeds" (John 12:24). Little did I know that this truth was going to be fleshed out in my life a few weeks later.

During the prior spring, I made plans with a friend to travel to Canada later that year. But as the time drew near to my anticipated vacation, I increasingly lost peace about this trip and instead kept feeling a conviction that I ought to spend time with my mom and siblings in California. It dawned on me that God put this on my mind, and to be honest, I wrestled with him. In the end, I decided to go his way. Past visits with my family were not always pleasant. Sometimes I had arguments with a sibling or a parent. Sometimes being with my family brought back painful memories. It definitely does not beat the fun adventures of traveling to another country. But a couple of years earlier, the Lord already showed me that he wanted to bring more healing to the relationships within my family. Even though I felt disappointed to defer my vacation desires, it was more important for me to say yes to God.

During my visit, my mother shared with me that she had been struggling for a while with an unresolved interpersonal conflict. She was deeply hurt and did not want to forgive. I felt compelled to tell my mom that forgiveness is possible because God has forgiven us in Christ. She listened and opened her heart to Jesus. She gave him her burdens and received his peace in return. She also had a change of heart and began the process of forgiving the person who hurt her.

God told me that my mom's transformation was a fruit of my obedience to him. Perhaps he could have done it without me, but according to the biblical narrative, it has always been God's intention to partner with human beings to accomplish his work in the world. Jesus told his disciples, "As the Father has sent me, I am sending you" (John 20:21b). We may not always understand why God tells us to do certain things, and we may not like it, but I learned from this particular experience that God's purposes are always good. Jesus Christ set an example for us when he surrendered his will to the Father and died on the cross for our sake (Matthew 26:39; 1 Peter 3:18; 1 John 3:16). We grow in trusting and following Jesus as we increasingly experience his love and compassion for us.

We do display a new beauty when we die to self. We are transformed as we allow the love of God to reign in our hearts and overflow into other people's lives.

For Reflection and Prayer:

In what ways have you experienced "dying to self"? What or who helped you in the process? What hindered you?

Think about any "fruit" that you have seen grow and flourish at certain points in your life. What sacrifices did you make to achieve or experience them?

Ask God what it means for you to "die to self" in your current season of life. Are there any desires, plans, or dreams that he is asking you to surrender to him? Or think about a recent time when you sensed God inviting you into something, but you brushed it off. What blessing may you have missed as a result?

The Enduring Oak

One of my sisters lives in Folsom, California. I decided to visit her family a few months after they moved to their new house. As I looked out the car window on the way to their house from the airport, I noticed there were oak trees all over the city. Seeing them everywhere thrilled me! There are only a few trees that I can identify from afar, and an oak tree is definitely one of them. I am always drawn by a sense of ancient grandeur displayed by oak trees, as if they want to take me back to some glorious past.

When we reached my sister's neighborhood, I saw a nice park and made a mental note to go for a walk in it during my visit. As if reading my mind, my brother-in-law told me about how they love that park as we drove past it. One of his sons often sought solitude there. It was a large park with a basketball court, a tennis court, and a soccer field. There was also a paved trail around the grassy field. "You should go check it out," encouraged my brother-in-law.

I had to wait a day for my walk because it rained. The moment I saw clear skies, off I went. Birch trees lined the perimeter of the park, but a large oak tree stood out at one end of the soccer field. Like I often do when a tree catches my attention, I got close to it, touched its trunk, and admired its height and size. I thought about a well-known Scripture passage, which Jesus himself referred to in describing his life purpose:

"The Spirit of the Sovereign Lord is on me,

because the Lord has anointed me to preach good news to the poor.

He has sent me to bind up the brokenhearted,

to proclaim freedom for the captives,

and release from darkness for the prisoners,

to proclaim the year of the Lord's favor and the day of vengeance of our God,

to comfort all who mourn, and provide for those who grieve in Zion—

to bestow on them a crown of beauty instead of ashes, the oil of gladness

instead of mourning, and a garment of praise instead of a spirit of despair.

They will be called oaks of righteousness,

a planting of the Lord for the display of his splendor.

They will rebuild the ancient ruins and restore the places long devastated; they

will renew the ruined cities that have been devastated for generations."

(Isaiah 61:1-4)

Turning my thought to God, I asked him, "What is it about an oak tree that can help me understand this important passage?" I received a sense about the endurance of oak trees. I wanted more explanation but didn't hear anything.

One year later, God brought the topic back up, at the height of the coronavirus pandemic. I was on a walk at Mount Tabor, a forested park near my house in Portland. The streets of my city were filled with people protesting the murder of George Floyd. My heart was heavy with this social unrest and the emotional malaise from the months-long quarantine. Being a first-generation Asian immigrant who has experienced significant race-related trauma, I, too, was processing a lot of anger about the event. I cried out to God, "Where is your justice?" As I looked about the trees and tried to get some peace of mind, I remembered my conversation with God about oak trees.

The Isaiah 61 passage entered my mind, and God spoke to me that he deeply cared about the murder of George Floyd and many others like him. As the psalmist declared, "The Lord is a refuge for the oppressed... he does not ignore the cry of the afflicted" (Psalm 9:9a; 12b). The prophet Isaiah also prophesied about God's "Anointed One" who will "proclaim the year of the Lord's favor and the day of vengeance of our God, to comfort all who mourn, and provide for those who grieve in Zion... They will be called oaks of righteousness" (Isaiah 61:2-3). As I reflected on this Scripture, I began to be comforted by God's promise to vindicate, comfort, and heal those who have suffered unjustly. Moreover, the trauma experienced by these people will somehow be transformed into righteousness. Justice may not come immediately, but the promise of redemption is sure. As the apostle Paul wrote, "There is in store for me the crown of righteousness, which the Lord, the righteous Judge, will award to... all those who have longed for his appearing" (2 Timothy 4:8).

After a prayerful meditation of Isaiah 61, I concluded that "oaks of righteousness" are those whom Jesus calls "the greatest" in God's kingdom. Their greatness comes not from their accomplishments but their faith. They are righteous because they place their hope in God's grace to redeem their broken lives. As Jesus declared in his well-known sermon, "Blessed are the poor in spirit, for theirs is the kingdom of heaven. Blessed are those who mourn, for they will be comforted. Blessed are the meek, for they will inherit the earth. Blessed are those who hunger and thirst for righteousness, for they will be filled" (Matthew 5:3-6).

Isn't it paradoxical and even ironic that broken people are the ones who will "rebuild the ancient ruins" (Isaiah 61:4b)? Indeed, God has and will continue to use those in the margins of society as vessels of healing, reconciliation, and transformation. People who put their trust in God and have persevered in times of unjust suffering are like oak trees. They have a strength to them, and those who are suffering gain strength from them. The lives of the humble become "a planting of the Lord for the display of his splendor" (Isaiah 61:3d).

For Reflection and Prayer:

In what ways have you been "oppressed," "poor," "brokenhearted," or "captive"? How does the truth of Isaiah 61 bring freedom and healing to you?

How can you offer hope and be an instrument of redemption to other people who are experiencing similar problems and difficulties?

Have you honestly confessed to God and to fellow sojourners your feelings about injustices you may have experienced? What negative beliefs about yourself may have taken root as a result of this trauma? I have learned a lot about confession in a course called "Becoming What You Believe."[iv] The instructors describe confession as telling the truth, which is best done in community. Being truthful is the first step to freedom because it helps us identify and reject the deceptions we have come to believe. We can then make room for God's word to transform our beliefs as we replace destructive lies with life-giving truth.[v]

Blossoms of Hope

Part of my lunch break routine was to go for a brief walk around the clinic where I worked. At the back part of the building were four young trees of varying height and of a species unknown to me. I liked observing them, particularly as winter transitioned into spring. It was a mild winter in Portland in the year 2020; though it rained frequently, it barely snowed. Come February, trees everywhere were beginning to bloom. At work, the branches of the trees looked like pussy willows. "Hmm, I'm pretty sure there is something important inside these buds," I pondered. Then I asked God, "What are these furry buds?" As you may have guessed already, I often talk to him when I'm out for a walk or hike and notice things in his creation. I never studied botany, and I'm also not the type of person to research every little thing I have a question about. I thrive on wonder; it feels very satisfying to have a childlike wonder about the world. I think God likes this, too.

As February was drawing to a close, news came that someone in Oregon contracted the new coronavirus and had been admitted to a hospital. All of a sudden, things changed rapidly over the following weeks as the governor declared a "health care emergency" in the state. Schools and restaurants were shut down, and to my dismay, church gatherings had to be cancelled, too! I started praying earnestly and met with friends online to pray every Sunday. We all hoped things would get back to normal after a few weeks.

In the meantime, winter blossomed into spring in full force. I saw more blue skies and welcomed the warmth of the sun. I went on many walks around my neighborhood, observing with delight the various flowers that sprouted out of the ground and tree branches. Finally, the buds of the trees at my clinic revealed what was inside them—white flowers with dainty petals resembling stars. They smelled like jasmine. How I loved looking at those blossoms, and how happy I was to learn what kind of trees they were! I visited these star-magnolia trees almost every day, as if they were my friends whose presence I enjoyed. I even told a co-worker about them—how the buds looked like fuzzy sweaters during the cold winter months, and now I knew what they were protecting inside. Being with these trees and seeing life burst out of their tender branches may have been a subconscious respite for my soul from the daily dose of bad news: coronavirus deaths, jobs lost, drug use relapses, political divides, and more days of quarantine.

When April arrived and the pandemic still hadn't let up, I felt increasingly sad about not being able to gather with my beloved church family to worship, especially for Easter. It was very strange to not be in a church building on Easter Sunday where we would hear people share their stories of meeting Jesus and experiencing his kindness, and then we would watch them be baptized. We would declare our faith in the resurrected Christ and affirm his transforming work in our lives. It was a time of fresh joy and celebration. I deeply missed seeing and being with my spiritual community.

In the very early hours one Sunday morning, the Spirit of God spoke to me while I was asleep: "Remember Joseph." God sometimes reveals spiritual truths to me through dreams. In this case, he was reminding me of the biblical story of Joseph,[vi] who was sold by his brothers as a slave in Egypt and was eventually unjustly imprisoned. Joseph spent more than a decade of his life waiting for God to rescue him. The biblical narrative does not say how Joseph coped with his dire circumstances or how his faith in God was sustained, but we can glean a lot from the way he responded in kindness and forgiveness to those who hurt him or took advantage of him. We also know that when Joseph was finally released from prison and had the opportunity to have a family, he named one of his sons Ephraim declaring, "It is because God... made me fruitful in the land of my suffering" (Genesis 41:52). God spoke to me that we all have a choice in how we respond to various trials that test our faith and patience. Will we be destroyed by it, or will we become fruitful out of it?

The season of winter, with its dreary skies and bitter cold, can be a form or symbol of hardship. Things disappear, die, or burrow under the ground. There are activities we can't do and pleasures we can't partake in. Similarly, during dark seasons in life, we may feel like God has forgotten us. Yet the season of winter teaches us that leaving the ground fallow is necessary for fruitfulness.

There was a long season in my life when I lost everything I had looked to for significance. I questioned God about why my life did not turn out as I had hoped or expected, but he did not answer me—at least not in the way I wanted him to. My faith in him deteriorated, and I started losing the desire to live. Despite my struggle and weakness, God did not forsake me. Instead, I experienced his compassion and mercy in ways I had not known before. He used that dark time in my life to enlarge my heart so I could receive more of his grace.

The coronavirus pandemic stripped many things from us. It is easy to stay stuck in regrets and disappointments. But I trust that when we accept our losses and allow them to enlarge our hearts, we will see good fruit come from our willingness to learn, grow, and move forward. We can persevere through the winter season because we know that spring comes after it.

So, when the fuzzy buds of my magnolia trees burst with pretty white flowers, I felt hope! Every time I went out for a break from work and saw these blossoms, God reminded me of his faithfulness—that just as spring always follows winter, he always brings life out of death, hope out of despair, and even good out of bad. Scripture says, "And we know that in all things God works for the good of those who love him" (Romans 8:28a). We see this truth of redemption beautifully woven into Joseph's life. At the climax of the story, Joseph told his brothers, "You intended to harm me, but God intended it for good to accomplish what is now being done, the saving of many lives" (Genesis 50:20).[vii]

Because God is merciful and faithful, we can be fruitful in the fallow and dark seasons of life.

For Reflection and Prayer:

Death or loss is a universal human experience. Recall and think about a time (perhaps the coronavirus pandemic) when you lost someone or something significant in your life. How did you process your grief? What or who helped you come to acceptance of your new reality?

If you are currently experiencing a season of suffering, how can you become fruitful in it? In what are you finding hope and life? I encourage you to seek other people with whom you feel comfortable to process your emotions and questions. Being in community during a trying season really makes a difference.

Epilogue: A Promised Harvest

It was 7:00 a.m. on a typical October morning. The sun had barely risen, and as usual, I was sitting in my car, parked at the Office Depot across the street from where I worked. I called that parking lot "my little wildlife refuge" because it was surrounded by fir trees, cherry trees, and even an old wild apple tree that still produced fruit. I often saw rabbits, squirrels, and birds looking for food among the bushes there. For several years, I spent about fifteen minutes with God by this little forest before I started my workday. I usually read a devotional book and prayed for my interactions with people that day. Sometimes when I didn't get enough sleep the night before (which was often), I would recline the seat and snooze for a few minutes. On that fall day though, I was wide awake. A maple tree standing in front of a hotel a block away captured my attention. It was so beautiful—this tree ablaze with crimson leaves. As I was staring at it, God spoke to me. He said that what he told me a few years prior about dying to self and gaining a new beauty is happening in my life again to a greater degree. Several months before, I sensed a leading to take a sabbatical so I could have more time to pursue my writing and publish this book that you are now reading. In order to take this lengthy sabbatical, I had to quit my full-time job in the medical field. It was not an easy decision. But after receiving a supernatural confirmation, I took the plunge – a giant leap of faith.

Sitting in my car on that cold morning with the dark sky beginning to light up, I sensed God's pleasure in me because I gave up my job in response to his invitation. I felt the "death" more and more as I anticipated telling my co-workers of my departure. I cried hard throughout the prior month, grieving the loss of so many things—a job that gave me a sense of purpose and a stable source of income, my daily routine, and my relationships with people. Loss is always such a horrible, empty feeling. But as I looked at the bright red leaves on that maple tree, God told me that I was not going to be empty. He will abundantly give me other good things to take the place of this job. I can receive and experience these blessings only if I give up another thing. God said to me, "I see your beauty emerging, and I am very pleased and glad!"

A couple of weeks later, while I was walking around the back of our clinic building, I came up to my friend, the star-magnolia tree, as usual. When I touched one of its yellow leaves, it came off the branch. "Oh no," I thought to myself. Then as I looked closer, I saw a small furry bud where the leaf originated. I immediately felt sad when the leaf slowly floated down to the ground. It wasn't merely a loss for the tree; it was a symbol of my own loss. But when I saw that furry bud, I realized that it is not a senseless loss. This bud is a vital part of the tree. I knew that a flower will eventually emerge from it, and I sensed God speaking to me again. I may be losing my job, but the master Gardener is planting a seed in my life that will produce abundant fruit through my willingness to say yes and trust him. I trust that you, the reader, will be part of the harvest. May you be richly blessed!

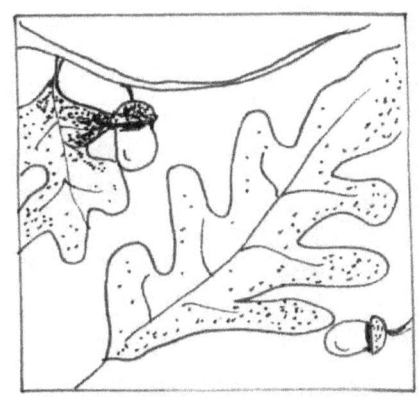

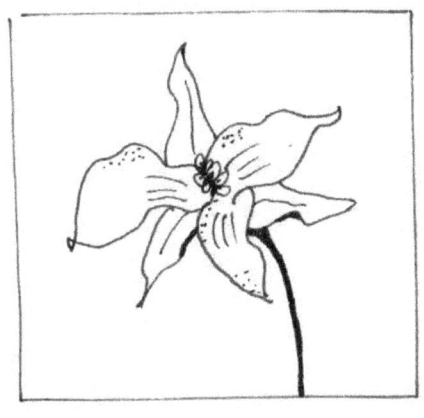

Acknowledgements

This book would not exist apart from God's grace, especially manifested through the following people.

Friends who faithfully prayed for and encouraged me in my writing journey:

Kalene Ardt, Anneli Anderson, Sarah Bachtel, Cheryl Baker, Mirjami Bergman, ReShawn Brown, Angela Braxton-Johnson, Holly Butler, Anya and Erik Chantiny, Kathy Cordell, Erica Davis, Linda Dodge, Lisa Everitt, Debbie Hocking, Louise Ko Huang, Michelle Jones, Rachel Jumago, April Khaute, Jane Leong, Stephanie Newport, Marcel and Martha Newsome, Jody Rutherford, Gena Siegel, Gabriela Trinidad, Lesley Warr, Kathy and Travis Wilson.

My writing mentors, Shelley and CJ Hitz, and the community of writers in Christian Book Academy. Thank you for serving me in so many ways. You are a Godsend!

Katie Erickson- thank you for being a patient, detail-oriented, kind, and generous editor, formatter, designer, and overall helper with my book. I enjoyed working with you!

Debbie Hocking- thank you for your professional expertise in digitizing my illustrations and cover art!

For my beta-readers Rachel Jumago, Kathy Cordell, and Mirjami Bergman. Your honest feedback truly helped me improve the book.

Phillip Stone- thank you so much for being the voice behind "Come Away", my supplementary audio guide. I truly appreciated you gifting me your time and skill.

My mom, dad, my siblings, and their spouses and children- I'm glad you are my family and grateful for your support through all the seasons of life.

Continue your experience with *A Journey with Trees*

If you have been encouraged or inspired by the message of this book, please share it with friends and other people who would benefit from it as well. Here are some ideas on how to pass it along.

- Write a book review on Good Reads or Amazon. Share on social media how the book has impacted your life and what others can gain from it.

- Buy extra copies to give away as birthday and holiday gifts. Donate to book clubs, non-profit organizations, retirement communities, etc.

- If you are a church leader or a book club member, recommend the book for study in your small groups.

- Your own idea: _____

Connect with me on Good Reads or my Facebook page "A Journey with Trees Book" to receive this free resource, **Come Away: A Guide to "Forest-Bathing" with Jesus.**

I would love to hear from you. Thank you for your support!

Recommended Resources

This book brought up various topics you may want to delve deeper into. I highly recommend the following resources.

Bonhoeffer, Dietrich. *The Cost of Discipleship*. New York: Touchstone, 2012.

Fryling, Alice. *The Art of Spiritual Listening*. Wheaton, IL: Shaw Books, 2003.

Hogue, Rodney. *Forgiveness*. Texas: Rodney Hogue, 2008.

"Identity Exchange." www.IdentityExchange.com.

"In This World You Will Have Trouble" teaching series, 2022. www.bridgetown.church/teaching. Also available at Bridgetown Church Podcast.

Mulholland, M. Robert Jr. *Invitation to a Journey: A Road Map for Spiritual Formation*. Downers Grove, IL: InterVarsity Press, 1993.

Rah, Soong-Chan. *Prophetic Lament: A Call for Justice in Troubled Times*. Downers Grove, IL: IVP Books, 2015.

Scazzerro, Peter. *Emotionally Healthy Spirituality: It's Impossible to Be Spiritually Mature, While Remaining Emotionally Immature*. Grand Rapids, MI: Zondervan, 2017.

"The Bible Project." www.BibleProject.com.

Willard, Dallas. *Hearing God: Developing a Conversational Relationship with God*. Downers Grove, IL: IVP Books, 2012.

Winship, Jamie. *Living Fearless: Exchanging the Lies of the World for the Liberating Truth of God*. Ada, MI: Revell, 2022.

About the Author

Joanna Montesino is a contemplative creative who expresses herself through word, image, and movement. She left her medical profession in December 2021 to pursue writing. *A Journey with Trees* is her first published book. Joanna enjoys crafting stories that connect people with God – the source of all life – so they may experience wholeness and meaning in this fragmented world. She lives among the beautiful trees in the Pacific Northwest.

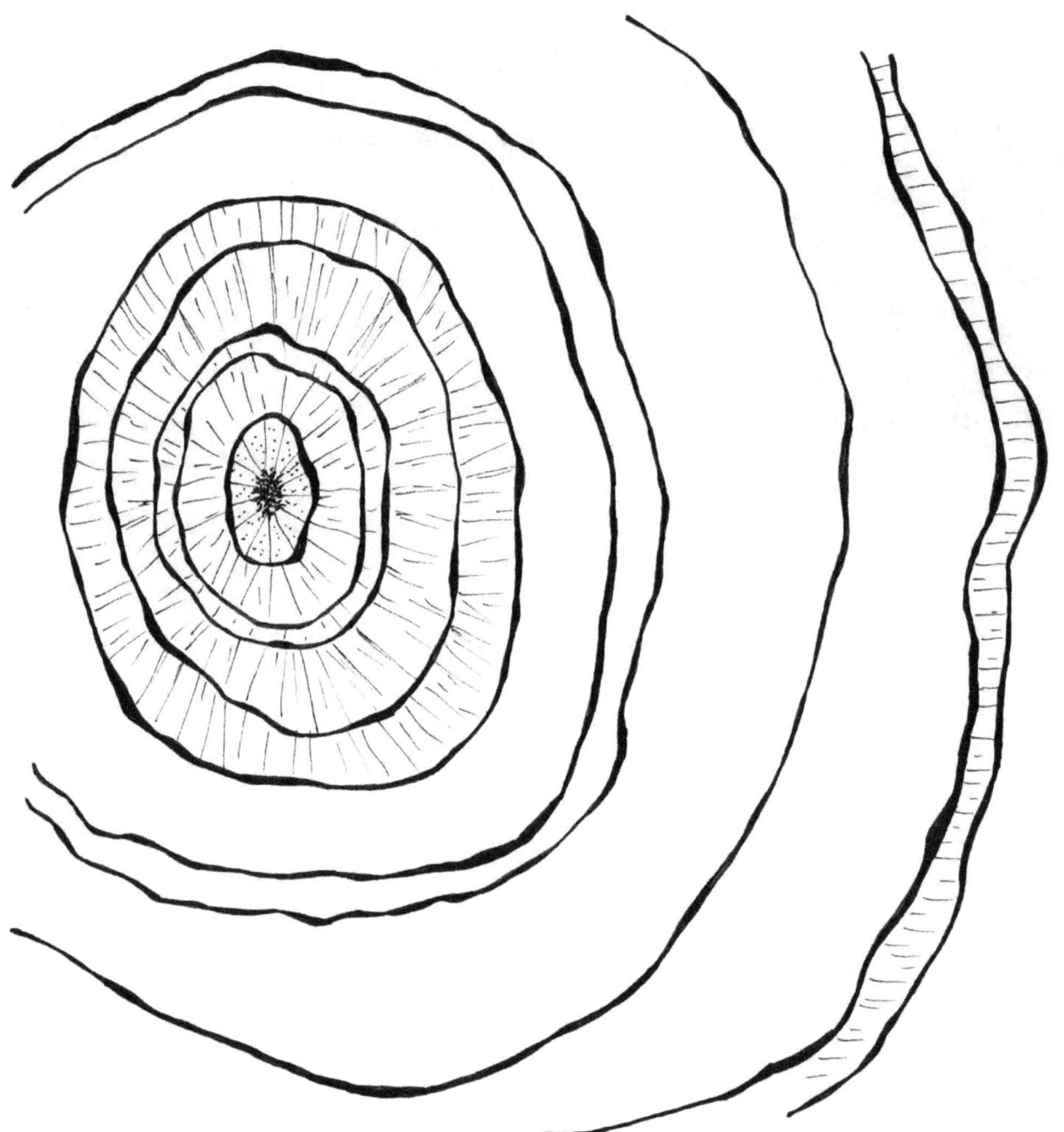

Notes

[i] "Heart Change" is a workshop offered by House of Myrrh, a non-profit Christian ministry based in Oregon City, Oregon. For more information, visit www.heartchange.org.

[ii] "Blessed are the Tears," #10 on Bryan Duncan, *Anonymous Confessions of a Lunatic Friend*, Myrrh 7016900614, 1990, CD.

[iii] "Healing Rain," #2 on Michael W. Smith, *Healing Rain*, Reunion Records 02341-0073-2, 2004, CD.

[iv] An online course offered by Identity Exchange. Visit www.identityexchange.com for more information.

[v] I learned these concepts through the teachings of Jamie and Donna Winship, founders of Identity Exchange. I highly recommend them.

[vi] Genesis chapters 37-50.

[vii] For an in-depth look into the story of Joseph, please refer to The Bible Project under "Recommended Resources."